Discomfort

Discomfort

Sarah Caulfield

Finalist for the Charlotte Mew Prize

HEADMISTRESS PRESS

Copyright © 2021 by Sarah Caulfield
All rights reserved.

ISBN 978-1-7335345-9-8

This book may not be reproduced, in whole or in part, including illustrations, in any form (beyond that permitted by Sections 107 and 108 of the U.S. Copyright Law and except by reviewers for the public press), without written permission from the publishers.

Cover art: *The Suspended Room* (2012) © Roxana Halls Oil on Linen, 110 x 120 cm
Cover & book design by Mary Meriam

PUBLISHER
Headmistress Press
60 Shipview Lane
Sequim, WA 98382
Telephone: 917-428-8312
Email: headmistresspress@gmail.com
Website: headmistresspress.blogspot.com

Contents

The Last Week of Your Life	1
The Tower Upright	2
ITHACA	3
Sapphic Ballad	4
Last Mass for the Fallen	5
Service with a Smile	6
Photosensitivity	7
Dear Oscar	9
The Letter	11
Some Kind of End Times	12
The Art of Apologising in a Foreign Language	14
In Warsaw	15
Break My Bones	16
For Alan	17
Kamakura	19
Shabbos Goy	20
About the Author	23
Acknowledgments	25

The Last Week of Your Life

The world warps and holds like a reality television show. Everyone is laughing.
Everyone is smiling. The fishbowl effect.
It feels as though I could put my hand through the glass
and touch the flowers and the stars, limn my mouth with champagne and tell myself:
I have always been happy here. I have no regrets. I have spent the best years of my life
amongst the greenery and all I see in my eyes are firework displays.

We are the bright young things of our generation but in my eyes all I see is the light of a
star just before it dies. We are the bright young things of our generation but all I hear is
all the air leaving my chest. There is nothing but a cavity and sugar isn't good for you.

They tell you you have to suck all the poison out of a wound. They tell you to put your
mouth to it and spit it all back out. They tell you this will save your life.

So here goes:
Leaving felt like elimination,
my spine curved back so far as I tried to lean into the grind that it became a wishbone;
Something to be worn to slenderness, and in all honesty,
Is it any surprise I did what all good wishbones do, and let myself snap?

Here goes:
I write with my head parallel to the pen, my wrist bent back whilst I sprawl horizontal.
I eat melon cut up so it's easier to swallow. I sleep with the structure of military school
and sleep for me is like falling. I don't remember how it happens. I forget: names,
words, where I put my keys, what you call an oven.

Here goes:
I have become angrier. I have become less tolerant. I have become less willing to excuse
people who mean well. I don't mean to hurt anyone on the road, but if we both end up
sprawled across the cobblestones, with a dented bicycle tire, dented pride, dented knees,
I didn't mean it like that isn't going to stop the bleeding.

They tell you to open your mouth. They tell you to put your tongue behind your teeth
and they tell you to make noise. They tell you this will save your life.

And here goes. Here goes. Here goes.

The Tower Upright

You're gonna go far, kid. We can all see it, we've all got eyes;
We'll follow you, eyelashes flickering like needles as you duck and weave,
keeping our distance when you slip in the blood.
Go on. A little faster this time, please. A little more coherent this time, please.
We're enjoying the show. You're making history by being alive. One more time.
It's not easy getting ahead. Ignore the corpses underfoot, the curlicue of the ribs around
your ankles. Think of it as calligraphy. Think of it as motivation. They didn't want it as
much as you do. It's a jungle out there. It's a battlefield. It's a rat race.
Don't worry. That's just a metaphor. The rats all left this ship long ago. You're safe here.
You're gonna go far, kid. You're gonna be aces.
We just have to get you out of this place.

ITHACA

It's graduation day. Five separate people smile and say these have been the best years of their lives. I wait for the punchline, but it's only me,

only me left hanging, left laughing in my gown,

Nervous breakdown on the steps of Senate House and it's all in very bad taste.

We are, after all, *Aristos Achaion*.

But people talk about Achilles' eyes alight and forget his bleeding heels. People talk about *best of the Greeks* and forget men once also called him *grief of the people*.
People always talk about marathons in metaphor and forget the second part of story:
they forget the first man over the finishing line did it because he had to,
They forget the first man over the finishing line died.
I don't think Odysseus ever believed he would see Ithaca again. I think he spent so long in the gold of Troy, that brief glory heyday of blood—price and tempered metal, that he never expected the gates to open.
I think that's why it took him ten years to find his way home.

Sapphic Ballad

A man says if you fall in love with a writer you can never die.
He's trying to get you to sleep with him, offering you an imitation immortality,
the reflection of you in his half-light eyes and
you're saying accept no substitutes *I'm the real deal son* as the director calls cut again—

A man says if you fall in love with a writer you can never die. Here's the thing.
If you fall in love with a writer, you will learn to retranslate all the facets of your meat.
A writer will say how your angles are blades in the light,

arrowheads pressing up from beneath the skin like a declaration of war,
and your hip bones hatchets she will flay herself alive against
broken open by the tide of eyes and teeth

She will say how you made her remember she had a body and you'll hear the resentment.

She will say that's what made her look the second time. She'll say that is the silvery yarn that dragged her out of the Minotaur's lair on bleeding feet and when it is over, she will craft a ballad of how hope martyred her wine-dark heart. It won't be remembered. It will be lost in the war, that's what I'm putting my money on. There's usually a war. Maybe it'll survive, but it'll all be in fractures.

They'll throw the bones like dice to make predictions about what she was saying when she said *there is gold dust in our eyes and we cannot see the sand running out.*

People will look at the parentheses which once cradled love stories and say: Take your best guess. Give it a shot. Go on, honey. If you fall in love with a writer you can never die.

Last Mass for the Fallen

Dearly beloved, we are gathered here today, in honour of those who
Burnt every last bridge, including the ones ahead. We anoint them with the ashes of
Their fall from grace, and remind ourselves that even up to the last hour, God thought
Lucifer best and most beautiful of his flock. May I remind you all that in striking that
last match there is no cause for condemnation; we are but children, and we are carved
from error.

We will now sing hymn number thirty four: *you are the best failure you know.* The chorus
is especially uplifting.

Dearly beloved, let us believe in a cure for the nights without end. Let us pray for those
who live on the wrong side of an eclipse and tell themselves they have not yet suffered
enough for the sun, who make happiness a currency enjoyed best and only by the
success stories. A moment of silence, please, for the drop-outs, the boomerang kids, the
all-nighter, full-fighter, half-bleeding-but-only-half:

for the kids who are told it will get better and go on into the good night on some barely
baked faith that it must be so, for the kids who try and swallow their dark nights of the
soul, for the hungry starving raging lonesome, the children with chips on their broken
shoulders, who choke on every feel-good story they try to take in, who are yoked so
heavily they cannot lift their heads to save their life:

Let us not make sutures a martyrdom, dearly beloved. All who survive are fragile. All
who survive are miracles. All who survive are deserving, all are angels up to the last
hour. There are no failures in this church.

Please turn to page forty for our offertory hymn.

Let us rise.

Service with a Smile

He comes by every afternoon on the dot. The clock turns three and he steps through the door.
He's slow. We have his order ready by the time he makes it to the counter, but we listen to what
He says anyway. The electronic till beeps. Cash jingles. Exact change. Every time,
I wonder who else he has to talk to, as each day I watch him eat alone
Out of the corner of my eyes. Nearby, I clean tables. Wipe up salt. We never speak.
It's been, what, five years? More?
I still can't hear the sound of deep-fat fryers without imagining him—
The quiet of his silhouette, as though cut out of paper and pasted down. Years pass, and
Here I am, trying to write with the idea that no one is listening, even though
I still want them to be listening. I ache for regard. Ambition's a bitch.
Words melt to putty in my mouth, pinned by my jawbone.
I am waiting to suit someone else. They're just words.
Can I take your order, sir? I spit them up sour. We are all in the gutter.
I doze. Drowse. Repeat. Wait for morning.
I have fifteen minutes for break. In the car park, I turn my face up to the sky.
And I breathe. Take shape. Let fly.

Photosensitivity

You keep asking me how I'm doing. I can hear it, supple
There in your sealskin voice like the call of a selkie flayed
The sore red underside to all your syllables,
The vowels little mouths, wounds and worry left unclosed:
You're asking if I've taken back up the bad habit of picking myself apart,
Slowly, carefully, an act of unsewing, a meticulous minus of love,
Like how giants grind bone to make bread,
Some kind of god-eating in reverse,

You're asking me if the vulture in my head is going hungry.

I'm doing what I can. I am remembering to cook meals!
If the warm ding of the microwave counts, and making friends is a—
Let's call that part a work in progress. You know how it is, moving back to an old city,
Where the streets all turn down to unfamiliar shops and strangers,
Replacements; that is to say,
Life is like watching paint dry, Lifetime Channel loneliness,
a cliche waiting for something to close in on itself
As enough, as a whole, as a closed loop, something that can be an
Ouroboros without eating itself,
I keep rethreading the needle each morning, a labyrinth of dropped stitches,
And sleep translates itself as an ache but

I'm doing all the things I should, I swear
But the light just doesn't love me back
And there's nothing I can do about that.
The incompatibility is something
Searing, something in how bones grow
Brittle without the sun but you can still die of
Heatstroke. Sunburn. Skin cancer.

It's a kind of unrequited love;
I am smiling at my therapist and I am able to save
Crying for the small dark hours, the safe and empty space that is
Easy in the absence of light. It's a kind of hoarding, turning
The inwards pull of gravity, huge in my chest, into table scraps
Tucked under the hull of my ribs, and you know, you must know,
After a while, you learn to see in the dark;

After a while, you start to see faces looking back at you
Out of the shadows, the kind of phenomena you can learn to call *friend*
Their smoky voices curl around like some kind of comfort
At least, at least, this part is familiar.

Dear Oscar

Oscar, we have to talk. I know we've known each other for a long time now, but
Oscar, are you listening? This is important. There's no nice way to say this, so
Let's be clear: I like you, and I wish I didn't.

I think you were a snob. I think you were spoilt, and careless with money,
and bad to your wife. I think you were vainglorious,
and that you should have chosen better lovers.
You talk about slim gilt souls, about grey twilight, about Hyacinth in Greek days,
work yourself into a tragedy,
ignore a boy who's been stood there, steel-boned since eighteen, in favour of death by
Endless Dorians; Oscar, I could recite your sins with the zeal of the evangelist,
and somewhere, unspooling down the years,
past bad wallpaper and dying alone,
I need you, Oscar. I need you to say *suffering is one very long moment,* else I'll never
make it to the other side of my very long moment, because I'm falling, Oscar,
I'm eighteen and falling out of my own body in the hospital.

I need you, because I am, deeply and laughably, not the boy you wrote your life out for;
Because where I am born, the air sings of salt and whispering Catholic kids in the
backyard, it sings of incense at church and me looking for one last saint to pin myself
to, because I've never seen anything bad happen here to people like me, but I know that
doesn't mean it's never happened.

I've never seen anything bad happen here to people like me, but at church, all I see are
open wounds, water instead of blood, the miracles of the invisible where nobody says
what I am out loud;
But at school, I keep my eyes closed in the changing rooms, and we all walk out intact;

Oscar, I need you live through Melmoth, through Reading, through all the bad editing,
Because I know how to say *help me* in three languages but when my teacher says *tell me
about yourself,* I say *je ne sais pas* and think of you writing Salome in Paris and how they
call history weight and I call it tethering. I think how they say *kill your darlings* but I
need to know I can live long enough to hold up the axe. I need to know that the way
I want women can be poetry, that it can be defiance, that it can be disguised until my
bones settle,

You're over a hundred years and an accent away, Oscar. Right now, you're the safest
company I can have.

You had to be infallible, Oscar. I couldn't have listened to your flaws like this then, back
when I was treading water. That's a lot of weight for a dead man walking, watching
a teenager in Cambridge, waiting for her to uncurl herself from your trials and step
outside.

So, I'm sorry, Oscar.
Sometimes you get so close to your heroes you end up on the dark side of them.
Stood at their grave in shadow, a stranger with flowers, saying
This is a break up song, Oscar. I don't need you like I used to.
I'm on the other side of the eclipse now, Oscar,
And even though all the sunburn in the world
can't stop me from carrying every last name on my body
a bruise is blood under the skin, a bruise is a wound rising
a bruise is the word *dyke* in the back of my throat and I can hear my history burning.
I'm tired of living like this, Oscar, halfway down to hell, lying with you in your crypt,
my own hand over my mouth.
On your deathbed you swore yourself to a religion I left behind at fourteen and I
understand, but I am not your confessor and you are not mine.

And I do not forgive.

It's beautiful out here, Oscar. We need to talk.
I need to say *I'm sorry*. I need to say *thank you.*

The Letter

Talk to me about how desire sits in you like a weight. In horror movies, they play music
Just so you know, so you know when something's coming,
But we're out here living without any kind of warning, you know? Just talk to me.
Here's the deal we're making: if I splay open my bones like spreading my legs, I'll let
you hold them in your hands. I'll let you. Go ahead. Knock yourself out.
Test the strength of my femur against your palm, just so long as you don't break them,
just so long as you don't tell me it's for my own good—
Even if it'll heal stronger along the break. I read that somewhere.
So for three days I eat nothing but salt, all my old hunger gone, and I chant it, self-
medicating like a psalm:
it'll heal stronger along the break,
it'll heal stronger along the break,
It'll heal stronger along the—

Hey, you know what? Fuck it. Who needs closure anyway?

Some Kind of End Times

i.
Burn-out:
Noun. Definition:
Reduction of something to its basest level.
Secondary meaning: *physical or mental collapse caused by overwork or stress.*
Informal.
Phrasal country of origin: United States.

ii.
On the news, they've begun talking about nuclear strikes.
The threat of being called back into dirt is one I have begun contemplating,
Idly, with a kind of distant panic.
There are footsteps where there were once children in Hiroshima.
At strange moments of the day—folding laundry, queueing for coffee,
I think about the ribbons in their hair crumbling,
The way lungs might have folded in on themselves, rendered brittle.
Death playing shadow puppets, over and over, against a rising sun
And the word we picked for it was victory—
But those were foreign children, and very far away, and it's not a cautionary tale
until you're choking on it.
And I think about how better poets have had better ways,
better words to gild the horror of the Earth we have built
but the lovers in Pompeii have never felt more distant.
Ashes to ashes, dust to dust: the devil is a white man in a white house.
It's a silly sort of prayer but here goes:
Not now. Not yet. Can it wait?

iii.
All my friends are dying.
All of my friends are trying to keep themselves alive.
All my friends are sewing themselves up with cheap thread, saline leaking all over the shop,
and I'm making myself smaller in the hope angels will pass over my door.
They call it *compassion fatigue.*
We're building man-traps in London town to catch the homeless out now.
After all, the only thing worse than the Little Match Girl is having to look her in the eyes.
We all know my government is standing on bodies, but that's nothing new. Look at the buildings.

The backbone of this country is made of transatlantic spines and people are starving,
but they're always starving, everywhere, and
I don't have anything left to spare.
They've stopped showing Puerto Rico on the television.
No electricity, no news: we're both being kept in the dark.
It has been over two thousand days since there was clean water in a city in Michigan,
but they don't sound like me when they talk, so I'm not supposed to care.

iv.
My grandmother told me a story once, about someone in the family
who walked back out of the war camps to a brave new world,
rendered lucky still to be in his body—
No, I don't remember his name. She told me he never talked about what had happened.
Language had collapsed in on itself, a black hole, a wound is an absence in the world—
All they knew was he was scared of the dark, and that each and every night,
He would put on his coat, the creases in the shoulders worn familiar
as the touch of tongue to envelope, something that ought not to sting,
He would put it on, wait until the park lights were switched off for the night,
And step inside. Over and over, until he died,
He stood there, alone in the absence of light,
stuck with the velvet licking of his own memory.
I don't know if it helped, all that exposure.
Like I said, he never talked about it.

v.
There's something else.
There's always something else, some fresh crisis to sink my teeth into,
Only I don't think I can keep doing this.
My gums ache. I'm swallowing down blood.
If this is some kind of end times, honey—
Meet me at the finish.
Just don't wait for me to catch up.

The Art of Apologising in a Foreign Language

You know, I know six words for the colour blue in English, and when I first came here
I must have stood in front of twenty shrines like this, glossy with lacquer,
And I saved my five yen coins for it on account of how I'd read they were lucky.
Every time I made an offering I asked the same thing and it was
please show me I made the right choice in coming here,
because I have never been further from everything I have ever loved.
It took me fourteen days to learn to breathe through the terror of it,
Dropping *sumimasen* into the laps of strangers as though reaching into snow,
unsure of but still grasping for the ground,
All my syllables sinking instead of skipping—

It's like my tongue's been taken out.

It's a matter of technique, that's what they tell me. It's a matter of time.
Excuse me, can I just get this please? Can I just get by?
Sorry, can you say that one more time? Sorry, can you say that slower?
I'm sorry. I know I'm a foreigner. I know I'm causing trouble. I know.
I only know how to say a little, but I'm trying my best.

In Warsaw

A man dies in Paris. He sends his heart back to Warsaw and says:
France can have my bones, but not my soul.
They call this Romanticism. They call this poetry.

A girl feels something die in Cambridge. She sends herself back to her hometown in small
And trembling pieces and she says:
England cannot kill me.
I don't know what they call this. Perhaps there isn't a word for it yet.

A man dies in Paris, and nobody points out this happens every day.
Death is not a prerequisite for myth. Mortality is not made extraordinary.
A man says:
France can have my bones, but not my soul.
A girl writes:
England cannot kill me.

For a moment they are both caught in the same hook, anchoring their blood's beat on the
unfinished commas of a still-rising chest.
All of the poetry has gone out of me.
They call this fatalism.

Break My Bones

I want to be able to say the word *dyke* without choking around it;
Without falling backwards into a smaller version of myself,
A decade old, who only knew the word crunched like an apple core,
Like something gone rotten. That it was something to do with what women
Did with their mouths, and that was what made them
Something unclean.

The second time I let a boy kiss me, I remember waiting to feel something
Other than fear. Nothing more than a cellophane girl: put your eye right to me,
And I disappear. It's magic!
Later, I cleaned him out of me, the slug of toothpaste winking up at me
From the sink, glistening until the taste was gone.

I long to arrive at a point beyond shame, but the road uphill is made unstable:
I am tearing out my own spine and calling it a Jacob's ladder, licking over the scars of
Old wounds so often they seem to open. They make themselves known with the sting,
Soft newly wombed mouths under my tongue, given life, growing,
Crying of holy palmer's kiss, and Communion wine, and the waiting reckonings
I have yet to make, the makers I have yet to meet, the growing sense I will have to answer
To my elders. Forgive me, I will say. Forgive me. I am still plucking out the stitches.

For Alan

There is a plaque to Turing on a building in Cambridge. Blink and you might miss it—
It watches, eerie as a peeled-open eye, unsleeping in cerulean memoriam,
Gazing over at the college clock. Time cut out into the petals of a forget-me-not.
Eighteen and closeted, I biked past it, and each time I felt a fierce kind of thing
Unsealing in my chest, some long-silenced organ roused and stirring awake. Beating.
Call it kinship. Call it kindness. Call it kindling.
I stopped in the great cresting wake of the fresh dawn, stood in the middle of the road,
Bike discarded, spokes wheeling along empty space—
Taking photographs of spires and the ripening sky whilst men stepped out of their
trucks, firmly Garbed, to collect the detritus of scholar's dinners.
I wonder if they laughed at me, but I can't blame them.
I also can't blame myself. I was drunk on light.

I don't remember when I started to point the plaque out to people. *That's Alan Turing.*
I don't remember how the epitaph grew so cold,
bitter as the taste of coffee with my tutor—
He saved the country, and then we killed him anyway—
as surely as if we'd put the apple in his hand.
I wonder if it was around the same time I began to sense, with an acute disquietude,
How much I stood out against the cream-limned walls of my college, a girl lined up in
the snow To be shot. Dissension in the ranks.
There is no place in the revolution of the mind for the failure of one
Solitary body. *I think, therefore I am:*
they forget Descartes brought that forth from his sickbed.

Here's the part I didn't mention:
I took photographs of the city because, despite everything, I still
Loved the city. I cradled its golden light in my heart, fermenting it, burning it as fuel.
One day, I may love it again.

The afternoon I walked out of the board meeting,
I realised the story I had been growing into,
Step by step, surrounded by reason. One letter separates it from betrayal.
The phantom mantle—of fox fur, meritocracy, an authority
Who cared about my pain—torn from my eyes, I swallowed salt, and swallowed again.
In a city of light, there could be no hiding.

It had not mattered that Alan had been brilliant.
It did not matter. They still lined up, slipped him chemicals,
tipped their heads away as he dwindled.

I sat under the plaque, put up once the patina of past sins had mellowed enough that
It was now reasonable to remember him. But it hadn't mattered—
Not in the most important moment.
You can turn the tides of war—but only until the light shifts and strikes you next.
It was less crying than spilling, a strain pressed upon. Overflow.
A man's memory a shadow at my back. It hadn't mattered.
I thought about dying for the longest time.

Kamakura

I had a dream last night where I met Trump, I hear him say, three steps ahead of me
In a heatwave. *It was awesome.* It's a word reserved for the Sistine Chapel, maybe, or
Rollercoasters, or a backflip. There is nothing lost in translation. The red of his cap is stark,
The color of a memorial wall in Berlin, the unspooling of names over red paint.
The resemblance stops there.
The greenery is bright, oil-heavy in the rising sun.
It glows, kryptonite, whenever I close my eyes.
I think of my grandmother, giving me a picture of her favorite saint for safeguarding.
I think of photographs of confiscated rosary beads, torn out of hands at borders.
I look it up later, to make sure:
Awesome: to inspire awe. *Awe:* a feeling of reverence, apprehension, or fear.
We all answer to something. I have to hope we all answer to something.
I make sure I am not alone with him for the rest of the trip.

Shabbos Goy

The soft seashell whorl of her headscarf,
The colour of a captured pearl.
Cut down from a painting, she smiles in my memory—
Something slow and Renaissance—
And asks if I will eat with her family.

I sit, spine rigid as a crucifixion, pinning all my words
Back under my tongue, just to be sure. Best behaviour.
I am scared, in that startled, understated British way, that something
I do not mean, capable of wounding by accident, will slip out.
I swallow mouthfuls of chicken, and warmed through by her and her husband,
Go back to the kitchen.

Each Friday, I dip in out of the cold dusk,
And never think twice about why they keep security stood on the door
During synagogue. A kind of blindness.

I see with my hands in this place.
I fold them through the water, around handles, and lift.
Pots part the sink and come up streaming.
It is a small kingdom, but it is made mine for a duration,
Borrowed in the strange liminal space before Saturday night.
I keep my headphones pocketed until the singing stops,
my head submerged in the sound of
Something holy I cannot unhear.

Soon, the kitchen will flood with committee,
Pouring out vodka into plastic cups and crackling with laughter.
The last thing I do is clean the floor, erasing the footsteps
Of every person who walked here tonight. Yom HaShoah is next week.
The first boy to call my name beautiful tells me this.
The velvet curve of his cap against his skull glints liquid.
The floor is spotless. I think of a pile of shoes, haphazard, to be wiped out.
And I can't breathe.

On Sunday, I will be thanked for my help.
They have no idea their kindness is saving my life.

Sometimes, walking home, all an ache, I think of
How there is still Hebrew song
Curling upwards into the air, outflung:
Welcome home.

About the Author

Sarah Caulfield is the author of *Spine* (Headmistress Press, 2017). She is from Blackpool, Lancashire, and has lived in Poland, Germany, Japan, and Korea, and currently lives in the UK. She holds an Education with English and Drama degree from the University of Cambridge, has worked as a fast-food server, children's mascot, art gallery attendant, and shabbos goy, and currently teaches English as a Foreign Language.

Acknowledgments

My thanks to the editors of the following publications, in which these poems first appeared:

Lavender Review:
"Last Mass for the Fallen"
"Shabbos Goy"

What Rough Beast:
"The Tower Upright"
"Service with a Smile"
"Some Kind of End Times"
"Break My Bones"
"Kamakura"

Headmistress Press Books

Demoted Planet - Katherine Fallon
Earlier Households - Bonnie J. Morris
The Things We Bring with Us: Travel Poems - S.G. Huerta
The Water Between Us - Gillian Ebersole
Discomfort - Sarah Caulfield
The History of a Voice - Jessica Jopp
I Wish My Father - Lesléa Newman
Tender Age - Luiza Flynn-Goodlett
Low-water's Edge - Jean A. Kingsley
Routine Bloodwork - Colleen McKee
Queer Hagiographies - Audra Puchalski
Why I Never Finished My Dissertation - Laura Foley
The Princess of Pain - Carolyn Gage & Sudie Rakusin
Seed - Janice Gould
Riding with Anne Sexton - Jen Rouse
Spoiled Meat - Nicole Santalucia
Cake - Jen Rouse
The Salt and the Song - Virginia Petrucci
mad girl's crush tweet - summer jade leavitt
Saturn coming out of its Retrograde - Briana Roldan
i am this girl - gina marie bernard
Week/End - Sarah Duncan
My Girl's Green Jacket - Mary Meriam
Nuts in Nutland - Mary Meriam & Hannah Barrett
Lovely - Lesléa Newman
Teeth & Teeth - Robin Reagler
How Distant the City - Freesia McKee
Shopgirls - Marissa Higgins
Riddle - Diane Fortney
When She Woke She Was an Open Field - Hilary Brown
A Crown of Violets - Renée Vivien tr. Samantha Pious
Fireworks in the Graveyard - Joy Ladin
Social Dance - Carolyn Boll
The Force of Gratitude - Janice Gould
Spine - Sarah Caulfield
I Wore the Only Garden I've Ever Grown - Kathryn Leland

Diatribe from the Library - Farrell Greenwald Brenner
Blind Girl Grunt - Constance Merritt
Acid and Tender - Jen Rouse
Beautiful Machinery - Wendy DeGroat
Odd Mercy - Gail Thomas
The Great Scissor Hunt - Jessica K. Hylton
A Bracelet of Honeybees - Lynn Strongin
Whirlwind @ Lesbos - Risa Denenberg
The Body's Alphabet - Ann Tweedy
First name Barbie last name Doll - Maureen Bocka
Heaven to Me - Abe Louise Young
Sticky - Carter Steinmann
Tiger Laughs When You Push - Ruth Lehrer
Night Ringing - Laura Foley
Paper Cranes - Dinah Dietrich
On Loving a Saudi Girl - Carina Yun
The Burn Poems - Lynn Strongin
I Carry My Mother - Lesléa Newman
Distant Music - Joan Annsfire
The Awful Suicidal Swans - Flower Conroy
Joy Street - Laura Foley
Chiaroscuro Kisses - G.L. Morrison
The Lillian Trilogy - Mary Meriam
Lady of the Moon - Amy Lowell, Lillian Faderman, Mary Meriam
Irresistible Sonnets - ed. Mary Meriam
Lavender Review - ed. Mary Meriam

www.ingramcontent.com/pod-product-compliance
Lightning Source LLC
Chambersburg PA
CBHW081509040426

42446CB00017B/3444